DEDICATED TO MY CHILDREN AND ALL THOSE THAT HAVE
CONTRIBUTED TO MY LIFE EXPERIENCES

THANK YOU

I have others to thank for enabling this book to be created and published.

Barbara, thank you for proof reading.

I could not have negotiated the complications of eBook publishing without the expert knowledge, dedication, and friendship of Monique Sinclair. Monique's experience is eclectic and vast in terms of commercial business in all its' forms and is available through her company Admin Matters (www.amva.co.uk)

INTRODUCTION

I searched for a reason to justify publishing these poems and decided it was my ego. I enjoyed their composition and sincerely hope that someone, somewhere will enjoy a word, a line, a verse or indeed a whole poem.

I have explored several subjects, love, life, war, religion, and nature. I know very little regarding the rules of writing poetry, when writing; these days anything goes. I have entered competitions only to see the winners writing about waste bins in a form representing RAP. I gave up and, decided only I had to be satisfied with my efforts. In my defence I have been published in a local Literary Magazine. This does not make my work exceptional; I know it is not, you do not need to tell me otherwise as I do not look for fame, fortune, or plaudits.

My words are often a reflection of my experiences and comments on the world we live in. A world that needs improvement, empathy, and equality in all respects. I would like all children to live in a world with religious tolerance, even if not religious and, one where we are all coffee coloured and of multi-national composition.

I am old, not too wise nor with infinite knowledge, however, maybe there is some wisdom herein.

Have a safe journey through life and when old a smooth transition to the next.

CONTENT

I admire a man who doesn't fornicate

Or drink and doesn't smoke.

But, when I think of such,

I never knew such a bloke.

Note

I do not know or remember if this is my work or anon,

However, it sounds appropriate. If anon, thanks for the sentiment.

SPACE

I stand in solitude, surrounded only by the night,
Gazing into a space filled with memories of time.
No one was here when those heavens formed,
God only knows how atoms and matter refined.

Countless Galaxies I behold, random, chaotic
States defying reason, they stay in place; suns
Attracting planetary worlds of unknown form,
With cosmic secrets kept from prying Saracen.

Those worlds, light years away, too distant for
Human span to visit, except in deep hibernation,
Suspended, sustained, in cold and liquid gasses,
Computer coffins, hospice of a new generation.

Silently they'll glide, in vessels bizarre, complex.
None will see the majesty of space, the passage
Of stars, eons pass, as does a life of Morpheus.
Their suited bodies will inhabit worlds they engage.

When safe on alien soil, far from earth's terrain,
If welcomed by empathetic beings, will they relate
The history of their father's faults, in all humility,
Survivors, ask forgiveness, another chance of fate?

Will I orbit another sun; see my earth from space;
Step through space continuums as time will bend;
See exploding novae implode to unseen black holes;
Their pull of gravity, relentless, to an inevitable end?

Endless time and space, black the night, as I alone
Look upon the stars; wonder at their magnificence.
Shall I one day orbit Jupiter, or go beyond my sun,
To a galaxy of planets, where life is free of avarice?

DEFINING LOVE

Come now let's be fair,
Define it if you dare.
Others have tried in vain,
Many tried in pain
Show it by your glance,
Does it eyes enhance?
Do they smile on sight,
Of images which delight?
A touch, our hearts stir,
Pulses race, his and hers.
Words caress one's ears,
Soothing worldly fears.
Lips form those sounds,
Endearments sweet, pounds
Ones heart in reply,
Ears receive another's sigh.
To give and never take,
Just for one other's sake.
Understand if they err,
Forgive, then and there.
Does a kiss re-tell?
Ones heart, all's well,
Or roses on display,
Proclaim a lover's day?
If you accept all this,
Truth, unblemished bliss,
Then, as defined above,
Maybe we define our love.

AFRICA, A TELEVISION DINNER

The images have returned, framed in a plastic case.
Pictures, black and grey, as lifeless as the horror
They depict, flicking through the comfort of our life.
The earth is barren, grass trampled by a million feet.
The trees have gone, burned to ashes to boil water
Taken from a dried up well, now turned to slush.
Emaciated people, tormented by their own kind,
Refugees of tribal conflict remembered from the past,
Now resurrected for the sake of a flawed ideology.

Hordes of flies, who are the only beneficiary of filth
Excreted from the pitiful, wasted bodies of the diseased.
Flies feed on the dead, the festering, decaying wounds
Of machete and Western bullets from Eastern guns.
The flies descend on young and old without remorse
To drink the fluids of life, tears falling from children's
And bereaved mother's eyes, filled with bewilderment
At what they suffer, for the freedom they are promised.
A freedom they once had, before the Warlords came.

There is no black or white defining boundaries here,
African fights and massacres African for pride of place.
The victory inconclusive, Pyrrhic as it must surely be
To inherit the scorched earth and misery so caused.
This is not the White man's burden anymore, except,
The pleas for Aid are heard by those seeing the pictures,
As they eat, sitting on upholstered suites, gagging
At what they cannot digest, on their plate, on the screen.
Two minutes of disgust, then hours of television revelry.

This is what we see; we do not hear the wailing cries
Of crippled children's minds and bodies, or the lament
Of mothers holding their dying children to empty breasts.
Nor does the screen expose us to the stench of dysentery.
Where are you missionary? Who once taught the Savage
The word of the white man's God and exposed him naked
To Christianity, enslaved him to white man's civilization,
Exploited his simplicity and strength for your gain.
Our legacy is there for us to see, all misery and pain.

Africa, the cradle of man, from where we stem, from where
We have not progressed, has God forsaken his creation?
As man subjects his weaker brother to purgatory,
So man continues to debase the work that God began.
(You have no idea what makes me cry)

TAKE HEED

I once knew a wise man, beard, wrinkled, old,
Eyes sparkled with kindness, many stories he told.
Tales related to children, sat close by a fire,
Warm in his knowledge, his wisdom admired.
He'd been an old sea dog, in ships with a sail,
Fought pirates, corsairs, shipwrecked in a gale.
Marooned, desert islands, where dangers abound,
Fought for his life, 'til safe sanctuary he found.
The man told them stories, many fabulous deeds,
Slaying dragons, giants, riding one-horned steeds.
Rescuing princesses, locked in high towers,
Of wizards and Merlin, with magical powers.
He told them of children, poor, orphaned, cold,
Living in countries, where children were sold.
No food in their stomachs, bowl, begging for rice,
Only rags on their backs, as poor as church mice.
He'd taken his food, his clothes from his case,
Fed faultless children, now fallen from grace,
Provided them shelter, from dead, lifeless trees,
Asked God for his mercy, head bowed, on his knees.
He told this to children, clothed, warm and fed,
Remember these stories, for soon I'll be dead.
Remember the adventure and all those in need,
When you are grown, succour, children heed.
Be thankful for parents and siblings who care,
Help save the children, all wanting out there.

DREAM

If I close my eyes, this world will disappear,

And in repose, I dream that you are near.

This reality, here, which I so detest,

Lasts not forever, forever at its best

Would taint my mind and ever scar,

The thoughts of love and where you are.

If I close my eyes, in darkness stay,

Softens then long night of every day,

Yet, too long in darkness state,

Defeats the reason and does sate,

The contempt, dislike of transient abode.

Accept that? No, tread another road.

If I close my eyes, dream another life,

I see no contrast, feel no strife

Between this time and future time's desire,

Because no fuel then feeds this fire

That each day smoulders in my heart,

End this despair, time proceed, depart.

If I close my eyes, it is now to see

In clarity, where you are, what might be.

In future years, I may recall,

If under spells of wanderlust I fall,

To be thankful for your love, my home

With you in England, no more to roam.

THE LAST STONE DYKER

The adder slithers to a stone the sun has warmed,
Scuffs a skin from its back on the Dyker's wall.
The scene brings fear and mistrust to the Dyker's eyes,
The snake is supple, lithe, easy to loath and despise.
He picks up a stone, aims, throws before it can strike.
The adder spits, recoils in offence, slinks away to its lair.

The Dyker slumps, breaths with relief; straightens his back,
From the depths of his torso his spine gives, then cracks.
He winces with pain, forces his back straight; spine reset
His tired eyes look at the wall he just built for a bet.
He stands there, tense, a hand propped on his side,
Feeling the pain of his age and the hurt to his pride.

The ravages of weather; wind and rain on his face;
Sun in the summer, have deformed his young shape.
He can't bend his knees or back, can't touch his toes,
God how it hurts; he could once toss a caber and fight,
Love and dance and drink whisky all hours of the night;
He recited Burns with a passion to the sound of the pipes.

He works whenever the needs of his own world dictate;
Bills to be paid, drink in his belly and food on his plate.
The Dyker's affinity's with his Bard, the hills and heather;
He's lived with the land, watched pheasant and grouse

Lift to the sky; eaten his 'pieces' in nature's domain,
Built his walls on the hills in the sun, wind and rain.

In thread-bare 'trews', shaped to the bow of his legs,
A shirt, long in the sleeve, tartan, in keeping with kin.
Lank hair falling on shoulders once proud and strong,
The last Dyker stands and stares at the wall he has built,
At the stones and rocks he gathered from a rivers bed.
He raises his cap, his spare hand scratches his head.

He sighs and he stoops and wonders how, how?
Could I have aged when my mind is clear and so young.
I hurt in the knees, my hips and my back give me hell,
My hands are gnarled, my joints beginning to swell.
But my mind's as clear as the water I gather to drink.
He weeps as weary eyes look at the lines of labours past.

Walls crumble as ages pass, stones return to river's bed.
Walls replaced by wire mesh; "thank God I'll soon be dead."
These thoughts invaded his mind, sharp as the flint and stone
Of his craft now embracing fields; walls built by men alone
He picked up the last stone, the last he would ever lay;
Keyed it to the wall, kissed it in salute and slowly walked away

THE MELANCHOLY OF LOVE

Love is an Enigma, not readily, easily resolved,
The puzzle too complicated for those too young.
Only years, each particle of one's heart, unfolds,
Till, when mature, your heart to love gives tongue.

Forget all that's gone before, 'twas not all bad,
Magnanimous you, forgive one so earthly bound,
Who erred, even when in Paradise, be not sad,
For in that past, now a lasting truth is found.

The lonely days are drawing to an end,
Single, sleepless nights, loneliness is past.
Soon, if you so wish, to my will to bend,
Promises of love, partnership, vows that last.

The years have passed; empty, less your touch,
But always there, a hope in heart, your love lived.
Time will tell if it did, time will tell how much,
Time will tell us both if loneliness is relieved.

If that time be now, then truth is truth,
I loved you then, I love you now that respect.
There is no witness, nor can one ask for proof.
End my lonely days, sleepless nights, accept.

ELIZABETH

Where are you Elizabeth?
I want you for my bride.
We met, I don't know where,
You now in me abide.

Elizabeth my love, my life,
Your face is so divine
And yet, I cannot touch you,
All day long I pine.

Elizabeth, I long for you
To my bed to creep,
And I go on longing,
Until I fall asleep.

Elizabeth, ah! there you are,
Running through a maze,
And at last I hold you,
And in your eyes I gaze.

Elizabeth, stop haunting me,
You vanish as a ghost
Slips, through morning mist.
A glimpse, that's all at most.

Elizabeth, be still, be here,
Where I can hold you tight,
I need you in the daytime,
Not just the dead of night.

Where are you Elizabeth?
You're really most unkind.
Where are you Elizabeth?
You're only in my mind.

Elizabeth, at last I sleep,
And by my side you seem.
I now know, when I awake,
You're just a lovely dream.

MY ENGLISH MASTER

He was big was Mr. Thomas and I was very small,
He was our English Master and Thomas taught us all.
Mr. Thomas stood six foot six, and he seemed to weigh
Around four hundred pounds, a fearsome sight to me.
The fact that he was Welsh, and in an English school,
Pre supposed to Mr. Thomas, we pupils were all fools.

He stood between a wooden desk and a blackened board,
Thomas lorded his great bulk before his childish horde.
Mr. Thomas taunted us, with threats, of what he'd do,
If we did not conjugate our verbs or adjectives construe.
Thomas made us read Conrad, an author of renown,
Mr. Thomas dictated, while we tried to write it down.

Mr. Thomas and I were at loggerheads from the start,
He made me stand before the class, Thomas tore me apart.
"What's your name boy?" "White, Sir," I shivered in reply,
"It contains an 'aitch, silly arse;" no compassion in his eye,
"Now spell 'apprehension' and exactly what does it mean?"
I spelled it with a 'T', for to me, that's how it seemed.

"Write it out five hundred times, by tomorrow White,
Now tell me the definition and you better get it right."
"Sir, it means to 'arrest someone', that's only one of four;
I'll define all the others, if you want to hear some more."
I did not understand the concept, so I'll put it in the text,
I was full of apprehension, at what Thomas, would say next.

Mr. Thomas had a favourite boy; he turned to him now,
"Newman, spell 'apprehension' for us, tell this idiot, how
We differentiate between 'shun' with an 'S' or with a 'T'."
"I'm sorry Mr. Thomas, I don't know, it isn't clear to me."
Mr. Thomas didn't know that Newman and I were chums,
Mr. Thomas roared, "Dismissed", we went, to do our sums.

The other masters, at school, were worthy of their name,
They understood our problems, fears they tried to tame.
Some were very strict, others, not quite so autocratic,
Some taught us very little, our knowledge remained static.
But only Mr. Thomas, was responsible, for one simple fact,
I never received one English mark, we could not interact.

Mr. Thomas, I think you're now deceased, probably in Hell,
For the way you treated me, it's where you deserve to dwell.
Despite the fact you tried to destroy my love of composition
And know the English language with its Global recognition,
I've overcome all the disadvantages, of being in your class,
For it wasn't me who was stupid, it was you, you stupid Arse.

CONTRASTS

I have walked the Rub Al-Khali in the heat of Arabia's day,
Where the sun beat down on the arid waste of burning sand.
I have worked in the heart of Siberia in the deep winter's cold,
Nothing moved my exhaled breath froze on a frozen hand.

I have dined with Kings in the splendour of Lisbon's Walls,
And eaten from their banquets, on priceless antique plate.
I have eaten, drunk with peasants, in places far from grand,
Their gift of food, plain but from a gracious state.

I have been rich, had money to spare, most I wasted away,
Houses and cars and jewellery, bestowed on loving wives.
I have been poor, worried, wondered if I'd ever work again,
Tormented by the thought, could I meet my many tithes?

I have been loved by pulsating hearts beating for me alone,
Sworn love in return, placed gold bands on slender fingers.
I have renounced vows to cherish until death do us part
Saying it's for the best, knowing love would always linger.

I have memories of a childhood, full of happiness and warmth,
Of siblings and parents, a family united well beyond my days.
I have, in despair or anguish, for my sins repented, prayed
That as I approach maturity, I understand my devious ways.

I have three children of my own, their quests in life, uncharted.
Will my past knowledge influence the courses they will rove?
I have no regret, except, I hope the hurt I caused did not mar
Those lives it touched, I loved my life, loved all my life's loves.

EXPATRIATE

Ten thousand miles my thoughts race
Through space and time, imagining
Memories of my love's form and face,
To these precious memories I cling.

Reason persists she feels the loss,
Adrift in time as much as I.
Wondering, if our thoughts can cross
The oceans, that between us lie.

As I awake to face another day,
She is not too long at rest.
"My Love" she may hear me say,
"Sleep, may your dreams be blessed".

At night I feel her stir, come awake,
Recall the warmth, the sleep filled smiles.
My hands reach to hold, to take
Her hands, parted, ten thousand miles.

Then my time for bed, empty, cold,
While she, the daytime yet to face,
"Alone?" I ask, not wanting to be told
If there's another in my place.

These thoughts, unwarranted, unjust,
Pervade my dreams, until each dawn,
Another day, brings back the trust
Denied by nights and all they spawn.

Once again, I think of her far away
And stop to ponder for a while,
The promises we made, each day
To send our love, ten thousand miles.

So loving, my thoughts I return
To her, to warm my lonely nights.
Each day, my memory to burn
In her, my touch and of my sight.

While her memory burns in me,
Distance dims not her tender charm.
Ten thousand miles or only three,
Thoughts never fade, nor idol harm.

IN MEMORIAM

Jean's Hovel stood in solitude, below a hill,
Open to the winds, that ever seemed to howl,
Bringing dark clouds that gathered overhead,
Enhancing the image of her Witch's cowl.

Only the remnants of the cottage remain,
The stones that formed the walls, scattered,
In permanent testament to its demolition,
The villagers destroyed her humble habitat.

The villagers all declared, Jean was a witch,
Blamed her, for all the wrongs of The Creation
The church could not accept, as God's own will,
Jean was banished, no absolution, denunciation.

No one came to see the Hag, they called Witch,
She lived in poverty, ostracised in ignorance, alone.
The cold of winter deformed her female's soft form,
She became the perfect witch, a deformed crone.

Her back bent, hands gnarled, warts on her face.
Jean swore her revenge, cursed the congregation.
Each year that passed, her image saw a change,
Children, even dogs, now mocked her degradation.

She sat alone in her damp, cold, humble abode,
Dreamed of her revenge, for all the infamy she bore,
She drew the sign of pentacle upon her earthen floor,
Lighted five candles drew a circle to embrace it all.

Jean knelt within the Devils sign; offered up her soul;
Bid she be given the means to reconcile her wrongs.
She careened and wailed her grievance in high voice,
Animals heard her curses, no humans heard her song.

She cursed the village people, the Minister of church,
Jean wished them poor harvest and death at childbirth.
She wished them floods in winter, illnesses to maim,
Jean wished them total misery, privation, until death.

Each Sabbath the village prayed and sermonised,
They asked for guidance from above; how to efface
The evil in their midst; evil they had all conspired
To persecute Witch Jean, in bigotry and ignorance.

The village elders met in council with the church,
Each member of the synod spoke of their concern,
Resolved to end the impasse, of Jean the Witch,
They destroyed her hovel, her body they did burn.

Jean cursed them on her funeral pyre of flames,
She called upon the wrath of God, eternally to dwell
In their hearts and souls; forever damn their lives;
To consign her soul to heaven, the villagers to hell.

The pact Jean made with the Devil, was for her soul,
And for it to go to heaven, if on him she did bestow
The consequence of the evil the villagers ordained,
They become his subjects, purgatory endure below.

Jean was not a Witch, she had been wrongly named;
She did no wrong, nor slander spoke of neighbours.
They all consorted to endow her with their evil ways,
She lived with hell on earth but resides in paradise.

The ruins of Jean's cottage exist until this day,
A corner remains, erect, structured to form a throne.
Some say she still sits there, waiting, 'in memoriam'
Of her torment endured, for her tormenters to atone.

GOOD WINE AND LIFE

Life is a bottle of vintage wine, fine claret,

Bottled from a harvest full of ripe promise.

Knowledge, processed by generations, then,

Confined in dark cellars, maturing in darkness.

Occasionally the wine is turned, the dregs,

Isolated in the depths beneath superior class.

The minders of the wine advocate their wares;

Its promise fulfilled when the cork is drawn.

The wine breaths, improves its' spice; only once

Is it free, escaping the bottle's incarceration?

Others admire the colour, fragrance, the taste,

Absorb the knowledge, contained within its life.

Perfection of short duration, receiving praise, giving

Pleasure to its maker, and he who drank the wine.

Then the wine is gone, recycled in a China pot,

Its benefits, the labour of its making, forgotten.

Are our children the wine? The sustenance of others?

Are we the founders of their knowledge and confinement?

Do we decide how the 'vintage' of the years are received?

Our children judged, as the Sommelier decants the wine?

FROM DEEP DESPAIR TO HOPE

When the sun falls from the sky
The grey face of the moon appears
And in the darkest shades of eventide,
Are your deepest, blackest fears so near?

In the hidden depths of the bleak night
When the moon lit shadows cast the shape
Of demons dancing on nearby walls,
Do you seek sanctuary from the senses rape?

One morn a Golden Sun will fill the sky,
And you may see a future full of hope,
That we can live in empathic harmony
With all the colours of our diverse Globe

I HATE TV

(This is vintage and of the time)

I must confess there are things I hate
And one of them is Paula Yates.
And all those who breakfast in her bed
Because they are so easily led

I don't think much of Cilla Black
She really is an old stage Hack.
And as for her series, Blind Date
There are better ways to find a mate.

Then there is that chappie Bruce
Whom at seventy seems too spruce,
He channel hops from One to Three,
That's two too many for hateful me.

Why do we import Aussie soaps?
Full of Sheilas and sun tanned blokes.
Can't stand the drama of Ramsey Street,
These neighbours I'll never greet.

The Irish, our homophobia invade
And on our TV screens they parade.
There's Wogan, Hunniford & chunky Holmes
Speaking in Irish tones from English thrones.

Then I object to children's hour
And this to me is an Ivory tower.
For all the brightest kids to ascend
And to learn homespun trends.

For we are white and Anglo Saxons
And welcome here all alien nations.
They should come here to be like us.
Be British, we moan, swear and cuss.

I could go on and on ad-infinitum
And specify many other items.
But if I do, you'll think me a grouch
I'll just crawl back --- on me couch.

COMPARISONES of LOVE

For too long I have loved so little,
Yet I have had a full life of loving.
The short years passed so swiftly,
Time now to record their passing.

There is first love, after you compare
Unfairly, those that come in succession.
They are not less in feeling, no less
Profound, just tempered with perception.

If we constantly compare the differences,
The value of our emotions is decreased.
Their regression erodes one's passion,
And discontentment replaces peace

Do not yearn for your first infatuation,
That feeling was unique, unblemished.
All its emotions without comparison,
Remember it, hope it will be replaced.

Isolate each new partner's excellence,
There is no betrayal if then you count
Qualities in another love, now recalled,
When eyes were blind to their faults.

For love is blinded by new passions,
At first you ignore and then compare,
The qualities of all you remember,
Good and Bad, of past love affairs.

Your love cannot serve two masters,
In mind, in thoughts or in deeds.
Only confusion reigns in deception,
Unhappy are adulterers, take heed.

REPENTANCE

I cannot ask each night, when I pray,
"God forgive me, for what I did today".
For I know full well, in my mind,
It was me, who chose to be unkind.

No thought of God was in my head,
When immoral paths I did tread.
Or coveted my friend's worldly goods.
Or, trampled flowers in some wood.

I did not take time to stop, to think,
Nor did I, from actions shrink,
If I lusted for another's wife,
Which caused misery and strife.

Selfish I, if children on my time
Imposed their needs and did pine.
Until I remember and text I see,
Suffer the children, to come to me.

If I know these faults and after pray,
"God forgive me for what I did today".
When do I need guilt or to repent?
If my forgiveness is heaven sent.

Better that I ask each time I pray,
"Take pity on those I've harmed today"
There is no fault in what they did,
Only evil, in my actions - hid.

So Dear God, if you are there,
And if you know this Cross I bear.
Of knowing the evil, I do each day,
Then of this remind me, when I pray.

THE SETTING SUN

Vibrant and orange hues from the setting sun
Cascade through broken clouds of early night.
The clouds move and reform, ever changing,
The canvas constantly re-drawn; Artist's delight.

Bright rays spear the evening mist in uniformity,
Never complete their cosmic journey to the earth.
The fire ball of the noble sun their stating place,
Their beauty; a Voyeur's reward beyond worth.

Shadows shade landscape, oblivious of its shape,
Highlighting a glen, the sparkling water of a burn,
Softening the outline of ragged, forbidding rock,
While cattle graze and drink without concern.

The sun continues on its plunge to Another's day;
Evening becomes complete as deep night descends
And its darkness hides the contours of the scene.
In darkest space, a multitude of stars, so day ends.

THE PARADOX OF LOVE

Hearts never break, they twist in torment,
Yield and yielding thus, our hearts relent.
The torment fades, as does the pain
And then our hearts are whole again.

Hearts bear the scars of past loves lost,
Ever after, remember, and count the cost.
Learned from experience again they tread,
On new paths, paths they once did dread.

Love is not an easy course, so beware!
The false passions encountered there.
Deceit, hides in Love's gracious names,
But also, beauty, tenderness, it acclaims.

The paradox of love, of loves and hates,
Given time, reconciles, and then abates.
Hearts adjust the mind to better things,
And life, tranquil, once more takes wing.

Heart and mind, re-moulded by degree,
They follow other paths, becoming free.
As the future, with each dawn renews,
Then the future, bids all pain "Adieu"

TWO PARTS OF ME

There are two parts of me that make me whole,
My physical dimension you can see and feel,
Watch as it develops, matures, and then decays.
This part can merge with other forms, is real.
A life's span determined by its environment,
But in the end, finite, then consumed in death.

The other part of me you cannot see, nor touch,
Define it as my soul or inner self, it is a thought,
It is my conscience living within my memories
Within the confines of my brain and its chemistry.
This formula I decide innately, never knowing how
I reason, hope, dream, shall be, or what I am within.

What becomes of this abstract spirit when I sleep?
Where do I go? Where do I abide? What concept
Do you have? Is my body secondary to this essence?
For the body does not survive without a spiritual host.
You cannot say the spirit does not survive its shell,
For this is not determined, this knowledge is denied.

Each night, each time I slumber, my spirit
Departs and steals away to exist, alone, in space.
Is it nurtured in a universe of souls devoid of adversity,
Then returned to stimulate my corpse at break of day?
From birth, is the intent to develop the essence of life?
Is death life's metamorphosis? When the spirit is free.

THE PERCEPTION OF LOVE

I cannot blame he that stole my love,
For he sees the same as I saw in her.
I cannot blame my love for choosing him,
If she sees in him what once I had there.

Who changed? Me or Her, for better, worse,
Could no longer stand the faults we saw.
Maybe we changed each other, unknowingly,
But having changed could not change once more.

'Tis easy to find fault with others' faults.
To rave, neglect those words of honest kind.
Better remembered are the pleasant things,
That true love brings to home and mind.

If we could forget the faults, be free of them
And comment only on the perfect aspect
Of one's love, that first we learned, then,
With easy passion, each other, we respect.

Respect is that one ingredient, of one's love,
That is learned, by sharing your love and life.
Achieve this perfect state of married bliss,
You'll live content, forever, man and wife.

MY CHILDHOOD

Childhood and the memories I recall, where to start?
I have a photograph of me, three years old, maybe.
I don't recall when the ' box brownie' snapped,
It captured me in shorts and shirt, on bended knee.

My podgy hands clasped a battered enamel bowl
Of huge proportion with which we fed the pigs and fowl.
The garden was huge, to me so small, a gooseberry bush
Where I was found Mum said, spread like an ancient yew!

There were 'pig sties', white with slopping iron roofs,
On which we climbed, jumped with umbrellas as parachutes.
There was a field of cabbages into which Mum drove the car
Not far away, a real forest with all it spells and fairy roots.

Our neighbours were country folk, scattered far and few.
Next door, they were old, had a horse on which my sister sat
And Mrs. Rouse across the way, kept chickens and a monkey
In a cage, it bit my finger, they bound it with Elastoplast.

A car, covered by a sheet stood beside the house, forbidden
To us all, we crawled inside and used it as a secret lawn.
My sister jumped from a chair at Christmas cut her tongue
She cried, lisped for ages after the stitches were withdrawn

We had a tricycle but sadly it only had two wheels.
There was a bag of sherbet dips that we all shared.
And down the road a shop of iron and a bell to ring
They sold wax chewing lips coloured the brightest red.

The snow fell one winter, Dad and Uncle Horace
And Charley what's his name, loaded a sledge with logs.
Dragged it behind Dad's Hotchkiss engine van too fast
To take the corner, up tipped the sledge, kids all agog.

I was nearly five, they said there was a war somewhere,
Dad dug a hole in the ground and built a cave with bunks.
I've got scars where Brother Mike pushed me from our bed.
He said sorry, it wasn't his fault that I'd landed on my head.

Dad left us for a time, six years to be exact, to fight the Hun
Whoever they might be, Mum said it wasn't too much fun.
Went to Wales and Kettering while bombs and Vee twos fell.
They killed poor Gran Sinden, alas, she hadn't been too well.

33

VILLAGE OF PROGRESS

In this green valley and these rolling hills
Stands the village; old grey stone houses,
Their terra cotta funnels, perched on sloping
Black slate roofs, billowing the fires smoke.
Aroma of burning wood, lingering for eternity.
A sign of warmth and life, man's presence.
Here we have lived, forever, with each other.
No one remembers of where, when we came.
Our time is chronicled in the register of births
And deaths, the masonry of the graveyard.
Epitaphs carved in stone, now lichen covered,
Placed with love, remembering kinsmen dead.

Stones and epitaphs the tourists now behold,
A Potted history; another instant photograph.
They see a memory, purified, of better times.
Look, marvel, at the past you came to see;
Stones of the valley, deposited by glaciers
Stones, Velvet smooth, the glaciers residue,
Erected as dry-stone walls, dividing pasture
Into cascading fields, retaining sheep, cattle,
Crops designed and planted to harvest from
Time between late spring and early autumn.
Those stones hoisted by men, loaded on carts,
Drawn by magnificent horses, long manes
Blowing in the wind, loads carried over fields,
From river's bed to village green, or distant hill.
Tracks carved from sheep's trails and fallen stone,
Horses hooves, consolidating the way to be.

A village community, dependent on each other,
Self-sufficient, an occasional foray to town.
The wagoner, his horse and cart took all day,
They plodded the road; manicured hedgerows
Defined the limit of the path; field and pasture
Gathered from the way and merged with distant sky.
The wagoner dozed, saw nothing, except a scene
Imprinted on his mind, from years of familiarity.
He would have despised today, discord, change.
Now in future time, a permanent road, black,
Austere, the horses and the carts long gone.
Those men, those horses, those stones, labour
Built the village, roads, walls; not knowing then
The residue of their toil and isolated rural life,

Would reverse the direction of their solitude
That lives and times would forever change,
Children depart, usurped by steam, and engine.
The roads brought the change, the motorcar,
Incomers to share in our dream of paradise.
The village is now denuded of its posterity,
Bastardised by design for others convenience.
Gone the blacksmith, tailor, shop, three Inns;
Now only one remains, partly a tourist office,
The brown signs displayed at the village ends.
Tourists come to see the past; leave the present,
Please God not the future; their garbage seen
On grassy bank, ashtrays emptied by a porch.
Todays' food packets blowing in the wind,
Piling against a door stood two hundred years,
The product of a craftsman, long dead, insulted;
A bulkhead, a final resting place, for rubbish
Discarded by mobile, mindless, urban louts

One road flanked by small, terraced cottages,
Divides the village, new lamps affront the eye;
At night, their amber light and unnatural glow
Dimming the view of night's stars and Heavens.
Remnants of the past, a China plaque, 'Smithy',
On a door after a sculptured, shingled drive.
Opposite the village inn, a memory, a weighbridge
And the village pump, in wrought iron, obsolete.
Behind the Inn, a brook meanders at its leisure
Toward the Tweed; crossed by a concrete slab
Bridging old and new; new houses, quarrelling
With the ancient stone and blemishing the whole.
The village changes; my Brigadoon, my Shangri-La
Assaulted, abused, taunted; I weep for progress.

A COUNTRY WINTER

Winter is long and harsh, in the valley and hills
A village reposes, splendid in near solitude.
Snow scarfs the hilltops, when new, pristine,
Cold, killing, covering fodder; deer, hare, birds,
Nature's children, starving, scratch the ground
Seeking the roots and seeds of their survival.
Frost turns running water to small glaciers,
Sparkling in the winter's sun, crystal clear,
Static, useless to sustain life, breaking limbs
Of careless, inexperienced young and feeble old.
Trees, providing summer shelter when mantled
With their spring and summer capes of green,
Stand gaunt, festooned only with the remnants
Of this cloak, now rotting; decaying flesh
Falling from a corpse, the residue of seasons.
Winter's winds cut through feather, hide
And hair, chilling the bones, now lean, gone
Summer's larder of fat to maintain warmth.
The wind strips the last vestments of leaves,
Deposits them on river's bank, in gullies,
On open ground, they rot, providing the means
Of new beginnings from their slow decay.
Winter arrives early, leaves late, as unwelcome
As a guest outstays the hospitality of the host.

LOVE'S FARE

Come! rest upon the pillow,
Head cradled in my arm.
Our bodies pressed together,
Warming to each other's charm.
I feel you ever closer,
Sheltered from the cold.
We sigh in contentment,
As arms and you enfold.
As warmth surrounds us,
We kiss as lovers do.
Arousing age-old passions,
To heights we now re-new.
There moves a leg, an arm,
Entwining around a waist.
Comforting the posture,
Of love, without haste.

Hands roam, caressing skin,
That now burns with desire,
Arousing all the senses,
From which we never tire.
The senses become passion,
Feelings become intense.
Now to love in earnest
In every loving sense.
Now the trembling stops,
We're relaxed, at peace.
Lying there together,
A time to never cease.
Lovers, locked together,
Combined, as lovers dare.
Fulfilled, in expectation,
Feasted, on Lovers' Fare.

PREACHER

The church stands square, spire lancing the sky,
Iron Pikes, joined at the hip, guard hallowed ground.
Within the confines of the fence stand the stones,
Carved in memory, recalling the history of the town.
From the church, a single road runs straight to Hell,
At its end, where one should find Saint Peter's Gate,
Stands the Inferno where nobody wants to dwell,
And where all those steeped in evil abide their fate.

Strange the church is the starting place to Hades,
The road is long; many deeds decide your destiny.
Choices between good, evil, come in many shades,
Wise men contemplate with care your deadly sins.
The Minister stands, perched above the congregation,
Sermons retell wrongs of evolution, offer absolution,
His tedious litany bores; learned by rote, his recitation

Without conviction, does not relay God's faith, devotion.
Is he free of mortal sin? he who preaches sublimation,
Who hears his confession, forgives his fornication?
Which turning shall we take? Who signs the way ahead?
Men of cloth? without knowledge of worldly temptation.
If there is one God, then God's creed is the same for all.
Anyone in office, differentiating between God's inventory
Of unity, love, peace and freedom to pray, does not fall
Between two evils, for there is only one, it is Hypocrisy.

Preachers shall not dictate, who goes to Heaven or Hell.
Ministers of the church, you are not beyond reproach,
It is not for you to coerce God into where we shall dwell.
The road to Hell begins, at the doors to your own church.
God did not intend you take his name to enrich your purse,
To be pious, unless you yourself are pure, without stain,
Which he himself absorbed for all of us upon the cross.
Preachers are in Heaven and Hell, where is your domain

THE STRUGGLE OF LOVE

I close my eyes, so cannot see,
There are no letters again for me.
Also, I keep them such, to hide
Those tears, that in profusion glide.

I shut my ears, so not to hear,
Those telephone calls, learned to fear.
Then, I cannot hear your dulcet tone,
In anger say, "Leave me alone".

I close my mouth, wordless stay,
Bitter words, of how I feel won't say.
Redress is not within my scope.
Silent I remain and full of hope.

I cannot close my heart to you,
The years remaining are too few.
With open heart, I endure, slighted,
Is my love for you so unrequited?

So, I clasp my hands and pray,
Send my blessings on their way,
Request you understand my plight
Beseech you to inscribe, "All's right".

TREES

It was noon and in the shade beneath the trees
Lovers lay and gently soothed each other's needs.
Under the mantle of the leaves and boughs
The lovers kissed and declared eternal vows.
They paused and rose from where they lay,
With passion spent they kissed and walked away.

It was noon and in the shade beneath the trees
Two lovers knelt and, in their hearts, and deeds
They knew their secret love would never bloom.
Another husband or wife would seal their doom.
They paused and rose from where they knelt
Their passion and their guilt so deeply felt.

It was noon and in the shade beneath the trees
The leaves turned their backs against the breeze.
The wind that struck them from the Arctic North
Was cold and sudden, a spurned lover's wrath.
Gone the residue of love and springtime rain
Gone the love that once coursed through their veins.

It was noon and in the shade beneath the trees
New lovers lay and soothed each other's needs.
Under the mantle of the leaves and boughs
New lovers kissed and declared eternal vows.
They paused, rose and parted with a lingering kiss,
Sighed the trees and boughs, this is not eternal bliss.

SEASONS

Spring, new life bursts from seeds
Dormant through the winter's cold.
Fields now green, nourish and new born
Feed from mothers as spring unfolds.
Summer, the young growing strong,
Nurtured by parent, warmed by the sun.
They leave nest and fold, so to belong
To other worlds, young and yet begun.

Autumn, mature, mantle of the trees
And hedgerows now in season turned.
Rotting leaves, falling rain, short days,
Gone the hope of youth, now yearned.
Winter, sunless, cold, days fading fast.
Chimneys vent, smoke lifts to heavy sky.
Leaves fall from Spartan trees, sapless,
Lifeless, waiting the final blast, to die.

It is my autumn; spring, summer gone,
Autumn matures; my winter's yet to be.
My life, I know so well is almost done,
There'll never be another Spring for me.
Could I pass on the wisdom of my life?
Spring, summer, learn from one's peers.
Autumn, reap the harvest, repay my tithe,
Winter then of promise, not wasted years.

HEN SPARROW

In the twilight of the night,
I spied a Parliament of sleepy owls,
While overhead a flight of swallows
Graced a sun kissed eventide.

Night passed and in an early golden dawn
I heard a youthful sound;
A host of sparrows, newly fledged,
Cavorted o'er the dewy ground.

The sparrows spread their wings
And fluffed their new formed down;
The sparrows sparred as sparrows do,
They parted and to a bough they flew.

Upon that bough the sparrows bounced,
Like joyful siblings on a trampoline;
Until their antics took them to flight,
My fledglings left; I waved adieu.

HOMO PARAPLEGIC (Where is God?)

Mum! Why have I got Spina bifida and a hole in my back,
why can't I move from the waist down? My legs are spare.
And why has brother Jimmy got Motor Neuron disease
when he's only eight years old? It doesn't seem very fair.
I heard you talking to Dad; what is it, this Testicular cancer
He's got? Is it the reason his sperm count's so critically low?
And Mum! why are there hairs on your face and your
testosterone levels are much higher and continue to grow?

At school Tommy's got Multiple Sclerosis, he says he's
losing his nerve, but he says he's progressing quite well.
Mary Jones has developed Leukaemia, gets radium treatment
three times a week, she gets sick, she says it's a lot like Hell
Tens of the kids have got Asthma; many have got short arms;
some have got stumpy legs, and lots have got rather big heads.
Their mum's were prescribed some drug called Thalidomide
but it really hadn't been tested and it affected the kids instead.

What's that man doing Mother the one with long legs and arms,
why is he running and jumping when me and my brother can't?
Well little girl he's abnormal because he's not like you and me,
soon we shall all be the same and he'll will be a spastic, extant.
Then the men in ivory towers, who control all the medicine
and drugs who make money for rich people we never see,
will find even more drugs to relieve all pain and suffering
they caused because they experimented on you and me.

But that's not the only reason; there's greed and ethnic cleansing,
chemicals and chlorines and PCBs discharged in the air.
There are heavy metals; lead, chrome that build up in the rivers,
from the factories discharging the waste they never declare.
We drink the water and eat the fish absorbing the lead and chrome,
there's no cure for tumours on the brain or cancer of the bone.
The poor die young, crippled in their minds and disproportionate bodies
while the rich live on their pickings and watch from golden thrones.

Eventually we shall be the norm and the rich will become the mutants
they will be very rich and powerful but have no one to control.
For in the end, when they have all the wealth, what do they ask for next?
They practice being God, a very lonely state with no one to console.
There will be one last man standing, with all the worldly wealth
emblazoned above his house for all to see, Croesus will be his name.
He will worship the one God Mammon, in loneliness and with no Peers
no enemies to fear, no friends, a world in torment, only himself to blame.

TEMPUS FUGIT

When I was born, I was helpless but desired,
I was loved, coveted, coddled and understood.
My incontinence hailed only with a Pooh!
When eating, my slobbering allowed to pass.
Encouraged to suckle at my mother's breast,
Cavort naked on a rug before my many kin
Dressed in matching wools, such a silly hat,
Paraded in the park, such a perfect specimen.

Now, as I grow too old to hug or kiss,
Oh! for an embrace that is not duty bound;
So much I miss; the feel of flesh on flesh,
A hand in my hand, a kiss upon my lips.
The smell of perfume I once admired,
The warmth of passion in freedom given.

Eighty, ninety years have passed,
Now I am loathed and despised.
My incontinence disgusts my nurse,
My eating habits encourage her to curse.
I am a dirty old man if I touch a breast,
Display my genitalia or milk white skin.
I sit in a chair in a faded dressing gown
Hoping, soon to die, being old is such a sin.

INSOMNIAC

I am deep within a forest where lies a glade,
Shaded by ancient broad-leafed trees.
Through the mantle of the spreading boughs,
Dappled sunshine falls between the leaves.
They turn and dance in rhythm with the breeze,
All in nature's perfect harmony.
I lie upon a bed of grass and buttercups,
Listen! There a pair of magpies chattering,
Woodpeckers chop chop among the trees.
Pigeons coo and dance then fan their tails
To say, "I am your handsome mate today."
I hear a murderous cuckoo herald spring.
Against cloudless blue, skylarks hover then swoop,
Singing a song, cheerful, oh! so sweet.
A covey of new-born grouse scurry by,
Oblivious, that on the glorious twelfth they die.
I hear the drone of insects in the meadow,
This I see and hear, my head upon the pillow.
Heavy eyelids, so near, so near to closing,
Will I sleep, will I sleep, I will sleep, oblivion.

CITY LIFE

Leotard women, Chippendale men;
Prada for her, Armani for them.
Red Maserati, Penthouse flat;
Personal trainer, Gold Rolex.

Grapefruit breakfast, Wine bar lunch;
Dinner at eight, Jacket and tie.
She's anorexic, slim as a bean;
Little black dress in which to be seen.

They work in the city, Private bank;
Swish new office, Pater to thank.
Nepotism at work, no talent of note;
Sky high salary, Bonus as well.

Decision process virtually nill;
Runs a department, no great skill,
Loses millions, can't pay the bill.
Bailed out by those from whom they steal.

IN PASSING (MY VALEDICTION)

If you think that I'm not here, beware;
For if I am where I think I am,
Then I am everywhere.
For I believe that if I have a soul,
Then my soul is free to roam
Wherever in the universe, for eternity.
Look upon the stars for me,
For this is now my domain.
Marvel at what you may perceive,
Every sight you see, sound you hear,
All you touch, all we loved so much.
The grass so green, leaves upon a tree,
Red poppies nodding amongst golden corn,
Fox cubs and vixen on a nightly spree.
No tears will bring me back,
Sorrow will not ease my death.
If this be true, then a part of me
Is of the sun, the wind and the rain.
I am a rainbow on a showery day.
So smile and laugh in memory of
All that has passed, rejoice for me.
Remember our love, our joy of life
Mourn no more, I am everywhere.

HOLD MY HAND

Hold my hand

And I will guide you through the maze of life.

Hold my hand
And I will shield you from all hurt and strife.
Hold my hand
And if I fail as you mature through life's quest;
Hold my hand
And comfort me, softly say," You did your best"

HOLD MY HAND (REPRISE)

Give me your hand to hold
And I will take you through the maze of life.
I will guide you through the mist and haze
And keep you safe for all your days.
If you take and hold my hand
So to follow me on this path,
The mysteries of life unfold in time
Like verses of a nursery rhyme.
When all this you understand
Then let go my paternal hand,
For you will be of an age
Whereby you act upon life's stage.
I have known you all these years
My child, now full grown
And I am reduced to paternal tears
For, to me, you are now unknown.
How can you reduce me to tears?
Be saddened by your unfound wrath.
Did I not teach you familial love?
Did I fail? Show you an un-trod path.
Tell me, where am I in you?
For it is me that's lost.
It is me that needs a hand to hold,
So guide me through saddened days.

FUTILITY

The sounds of war are not the bullets' whine,
Nor are they the bursting shells.
The sounds of war are the orphans' cries
As they learn to survive a living hell.

The sights of war are not the burning tanks,
Nor are they the dark smoke laden skies.
The sights of war are the maimed and dead,
Smouldering embers on a funeral pyre.

The smells of war are not the cordite fumes,
Nor are they the stench of scorching earth.
The smells of war are the festering wounds,
Rotting flesh coupled with throes of death.

The feel of war is not recoiling rifle' butts,
Nor is it the pain of severed legs and arms.
The feel of war is the sorrow of kinsmen dead,
And the void of broken hearts that harm.

The voice of war is not the cheering battle cry,
Nor is it the singing of the Sovereign's hymn.
The voice of war MUST be the Media's claim,
That the carnage and the dead are all in vain.

The sixth sense of war is not sub-conscious
Thoughts that we shall survive and win.
The sixth sense of war is the thoughtful
Claim that conflict is a Mortal sin.

NO REGRETS

Life progresses and years accrue
Wisdom and knowledge also do.
But early memories fade and blur,
They wane, as does the moon.

Unlike the moon that waxes full,
Our memories do not renew.
They forever linger as shadows,
Ghostly spectres of fading youth.

Childhood becomes a distant past
As four times twenty years unfold.
We remember sunshine, not the rain;
What the future holds remains untold.

We regret things that remain undone.
Loves lost, loves we can't renew.
Deeds we should have strived to do
And deeds we wish not to review.

As we mature, time's race accelerates,
So we stumble towards our final breath.
Once a long-term formless thought,
A Tape stretched twixt life and death.

With one last breath we breast the Tape
Our time and memories have now elapsed
What does the future hold?
Unknown, unfettered, endless possibilities.

Printed in Great Britain
by Amazon

39712425R00030